AF285422

CLAUDIA SCHRÖDER, BERND OESTEREICH

Werkstatt
für kollegiale Führung

Be excellent to each other

Chaos Computer Club

THE ROLE
OF PROCESS,
STRUCTURE
AND
ATTITUDE
IN
COLLEGIAL
LEADERSHIP

The collegial model of
organisational development is
an evolutionary approach which
- in contrast to other processes
of change - may nevertheless
have revolutionary effects.

The model comprises numerous
incremental small-step alternatives
to abrupt, wholesale change in
the organisation of leadership
which are attuned to a business'
culture, temporal circumstances
and the needs of colleagues.

In this book we would like to describe the following six basic elements in more detail:

1) The **PROFESSIONAL SYSTEMIC-INTEGRAL BEHAVIOUR** of external consultants who support the company and the willingness of the client to adapt them.

2) **A SMALL-STEP APPROACH** that is geared to the potential tempo of change within the organisation and that can co-exist with existing management systems on a transitional or permanent basis rather than abruptly replacing such systems in their entirety.

3) **COLLEGIAL LEADERSHIP**, i.e. distributed leadership based on the **PULL-PRINCIPLE**, instead of change stipulated from above according to the push-principle.

4) **DIALOGICAL PROCESS DEVELOPMENT** with various moderated communication and dialogue formats that facilitate a feedback culture in which consultants act as learning guides.

5) **A CLEAR FRAMEWORK** that unambiguously differentiates between the collegial framework and non-challengeable leadership responsibilities.

6) **CLEAR INITIAL INTERNAL STRUCTURE AND PROCESS GUIDELINES** which enable colleagues to get started on self-organisation immediately without being overwhelmed by ill-defined and entirely open-ended aims which also require extensive training.

CONTENT

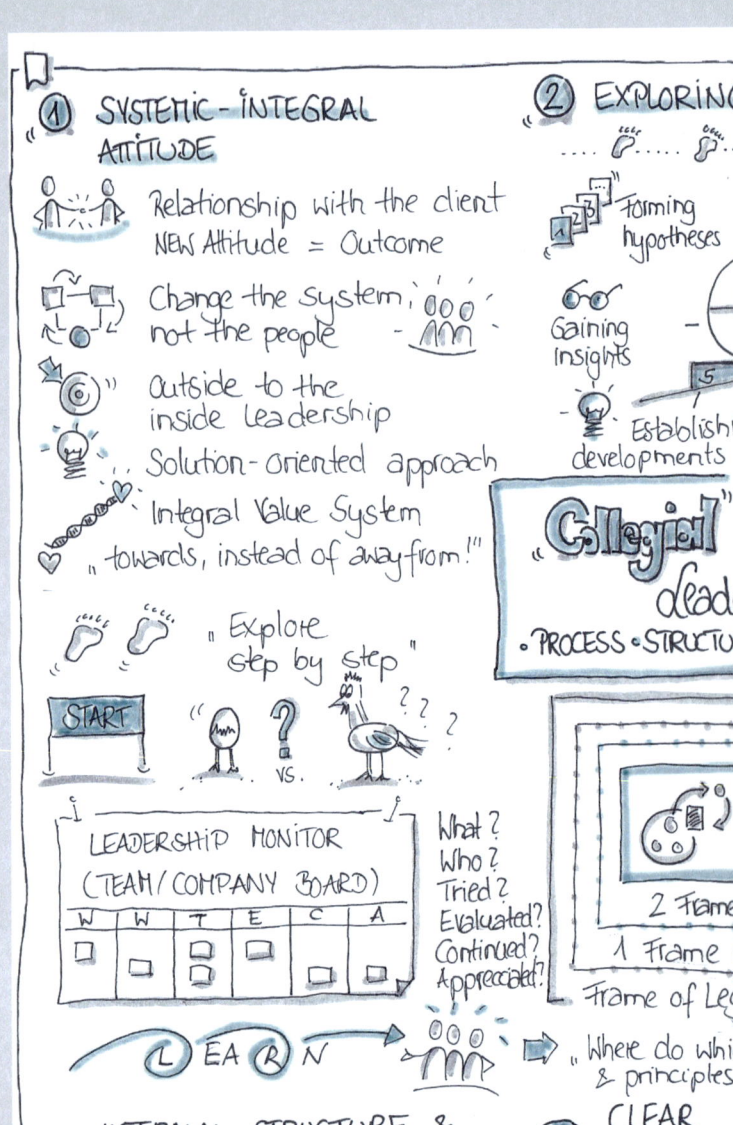

① SYSTEMIC - INTEGRAL ATTITUDE

Relationship with the client
NEW Attitude = Outcome

Change the system, not the people

Outside to the inside Leadership

Solution-oriented approach

Integral Value System
„towards, instead of away from!"

„Explore step by step"

START

VS.

LEADERSHIP MONITOR
(TEAM / COMPANY BOARD)

W	W	T	E	C	A
☐	☐	☐	☐	☐	☐

What?
Who?
Tried?
Evaluated?
Continued?
Appreciated?

L EA R N

② EXPLORING

Forming hypotheses

Gaining insights

Establishing developments

Collegial leade
• PROCESS • STRUCTU

2 Frame
1 Frame
Frame of Leg

„Where do whic & principles

⑥ INTERNAL STRUCTURE & PROCESS SPECIFICATIONS

⑤ CLEAR FRAMEWOR

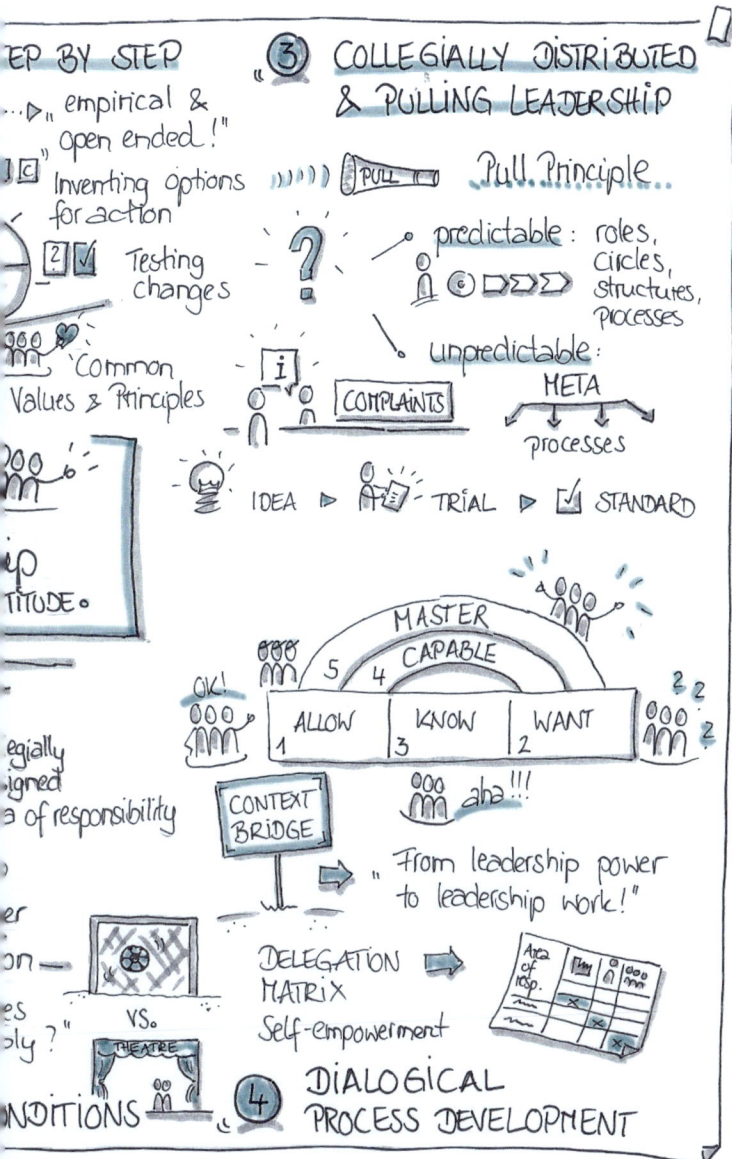

EP BY STEP

...▷ "empirical & open ended!"

1 C "Inventing options for action"

2 ✓ Testing changes

Common Values & Principles

...IP ...TITUDE.

...egially ...igned ...e of responsibility

...er

...on —

...es ...ly?"

...NDITIONS

VS.

THEATRE

"③ COLLEGIALLY DISTRIBUTED & PULLING LEADERSHIP

))))) [PULL] Pull Principle...

predictable: roles, circles, structures, processes

unpredictable: META ↓ ↓ ↓ processes

? COMPLAINTS

IDEA ▷ TRIAL ▷ ✓ STANDARD

MASTER
CAPABLE

	5	4	
ALLOW	KNOW	WANT
1	3	2

OK!

2 2 2

CONTEXT BRIDGE

aha!!!

⇨ "From leadership power to leadership work!"

DELEGATION MATRIX ⇨
Self-empowerment

Area of resp. | Tim | | doo something

④ DIALOGICAL PROCESS DEVELOPMENT

content: Bernd Oestereich & Claudia Schröder / Sketchnote: Heike Heeg

1

A PROFESSIONAL SYSTEMIC-INTEGRAL ATTITUDE

We understand attitude as being a specific inner breakpoint consisting of values, insights, thought patterns and emotional patterns in a concrete context that guides our behaviour. An attitude is therefore not merely a conviction or personal bias - it is observable in the individual life process, i.e. in a person's actions, objectives, statements and judgements. It is a bridge between internalised theory and emotional patterns to practice and ability. Attitudes can be learned and are therefore also part of professional personality development in a work context.

THE RELATIONSHIP WITH THE CLIENT IN THE CONTEXT OF A PROFESSIONAL ATTITUDE

As a rule, the client and the members of the organisation do not yet have the desired attitude: if they did, they would not need our support as learning guide or consultants. A new attitude is therefore not the prerequisite for agile organisational development but its outcome. The client and it's organisational members may have knowledge of agile and collegial values and possibly also of individual experiences. However, they do not usually yet have the attitude in the shape of certain values, insights, thought and feeling patterns which would give the stakeholders support and safety in their actions.

Our main task as external companions in the real organisational context is to make certain attitudes practicable (trainable) and to demonstrate them with great clarity. In this context, an organisation's traditional values will always be in conflict with those of agile organisational development. Stakeholders will also continue to resort back to old patterns of behaviour in the adaptation process. Our task as consultants is to identify these differences, including incipient changes, and to make them clearly perceptible for the members of the organisation.

Consultants require more than just process competence if they are to achieve this. They also need resilient specialist knowledge of agile organisational development which they can use to flag up these differences and emerging developments.

What are the relevant attitudes?

In the following we identify the values and attitudes which we regard as important. We are aware that this is a subjective and incomplete enumeration. In view of the scope of this book, we will simply name these values and attitudes briefly rather than describing them in detail.

CHANGE THE SYSTEM, NOT THE PEOPLE.

A systemic-constructivist attitude is one in which each person acts in a meaningful way from his or her point of view in each moment and context. Human beings are social beings and human existence is only viable collectively. We naturally strive to integrate ourselves into groups, to make valuable contributions and to obtain recognition.

At the same time people are complex beings with different needs, emotions, values, selective perceptions and their own individual constructions of reality. It is therefore impossible to fully interpret, control or predict our behaviour from the outside. Recognition of the integrity of each member of an organisation is one of the basic principles of agile organisational development. The aim is not to adapt people's behaviour to meet certain goals, but rather to create new communication practices, processes and structures that make it easier for people to compare their own image with that of others and to test new ways of acting in order to be able to develop further.

OUTSIDE TO THE INSIDE LEADERSHIP

In order to adapt, organisations need the most direct connection possible to and resonance with the environment, especially to the market. The agile organisation is therefore led from the outside inwards. Direct value creation is located on the periphery, i.e. on the border with the market. It is not the headquarters, but the units on the periphery that make decisions affecting value creation and everything related to it (products, prices, business models, strategies, suppliers, internal supplier services, own personnel, etc.)

SOLUTION-ORIENTED APPROACH

We are guided by the following common systemic principles:

- We focus our attention as much as possible on solutions, possibilities and opportunities and as little as necessary on problems, deficits or deficiencies.

- We focus on supporters rather than on resistances and reservations.

- We facilitate new behaviours rather than prevent existing ones.

- We simply try achieving something within a manageable framework rather than speculating or seeking reassurance about the potential effects or benefits of our decisions and actions.

- We appreciate what is and how it came about. We try to understand the usefulness of existing adversities in an appreciative way, rather than considering them mere burdens.

- We strive for multiple perspectives rather than generalisations.

- We calmly trust the members of the organisation.

INTEGRAL VALUE SYSTEM: TOWARDS INSTEAD OF AWAY FROM

Integral models such as Spiral Dynamics describe and distinguish certain value systems. These value systems show a long-term trend towards steadily increasing complexity and connectedness. All value systems are concerned with the creation of security and the survival of individuals and communities.

While first-order level value systems in Spiral Dynamics (beige to green) are essentially about moving away from subsistence; second-order value systems (yellow and turquoise) are characterized by abundance and richness and a moving towards.

We consider second-order level value systems to be important in the context of agile organisational development. Our model is based on movement forward and integral value systems. In our opinion, the requirements for adaptability in a complex and dynamic environment are easier to meet within an integral value system.

The second-order level is also concerned with survival and development of life, ecosystems and the planet itself, i.e. humanity, animals and plants. In the context of organisations and companies, the interactions and interconnectedness of social systems with their environment are therefore of relevance. Only through new thought structures and approaches will we be able to make mature transcontextual decisions.

- What benefits does an organisation generate for society?

- What contribution does it make to the development of society and the planet? How do we deal with resources?

The higher evolutionary sense of the yellow level of Spiral Dynamics has also become more significant as a result of current technologies. We have created a global system based on the Internet and an unprecedented all-connectedness.

Devices, living beings, organisations and societies of all kinds are interconnected in a variety of ways. We have thus reached a completely new dimension of complexity and dynamics. This raises questions of responsibility and the common good. Interactions on a planetary scale also move to the centre of attention. It literally pulls us into the yellow.

This pull is overwhelming value systems which are geared to overcoming subsistence. We regard agile organisational development as part of a second-order value system that uses existing resources to create a more integral future. We therefore regard clarifying why, where to, and higher evolutionary purpose as an obligatory element.

dynamic →

Use Cases and Context

Reproducible and resettable system behaviour
Different Implementation Contexts (Development, Test, Production)
Test- and Build Automatisation, Configuration Management
Development as main activity and direct value added

←

LeSS, SAFe etc.

Scrum

Lean, Software-Kanban

DoD-STD-2167, CMMI etc.

Waterfallmodel

← stable

← Technical Systems (causal)   *Development*

evelopment Models

Work on the running, living and non-exchangeable system
(not resettable, not reproducible, not virtualizable)
System consists of contingent social communications
Development parallel to actual value added

➜

**Collegial-selforganised
agile Organisation Development**

**Open-ended systemic
Organisation Development**

Moving
Targets

Sociocracy

Fixed
Targets

Holocracy

**Target-oriented
Change-Management**

Kommerzielle Nutzung bei Nennung des Rechteinhabers erlaubt:
Bernd Oestereich, Claudia Schröder (https://kollegiale-fuehrung.de)

ject (Object)   **Social Systems (complex) ➜**

2

MOVING FORWARD AND EXPLORING STEP BY STEP

The agile OE loop which we have developed (see illustration on next page) is a synthesis of PDCA circuit (whose predecessor was developed by Walter A. Shewart as early as 1930 [W. E. Deming: Out of the Crisis; Massachusetts Institute of Technology, Cambridge, 1982]) and the systemic loop [Roswita Königswieser, Alexander Exner: Systemische Intervention - Architekturen und Designs für Berater und Veränderungsmanager, Stuttgart 1998] supplemented by the integration and standardisation (visualised as a wedge) of prototypical developments, a common basis of values and principles, and loose association with the levels (colours) of Spiral Dynamics.

1. GAINING INSIGHTS

The process begins by gaining information about the object of observation. If possible, we visualise this information without evaluating it.

2. FORMING HYPOTHESES

We then form hypotheses, i.e. assumptions about possible cause-effect relationships. In a constructivist manner, we form potential constructions of reality that are understood as equally valid perspectives. In contrast to Scrum's usual PDCA cycle, with its distinctions of right/wrong or finished/unfinished, we instead form an opinion about how helpful the resulting hypotheses and views might be for our goals and concerns.

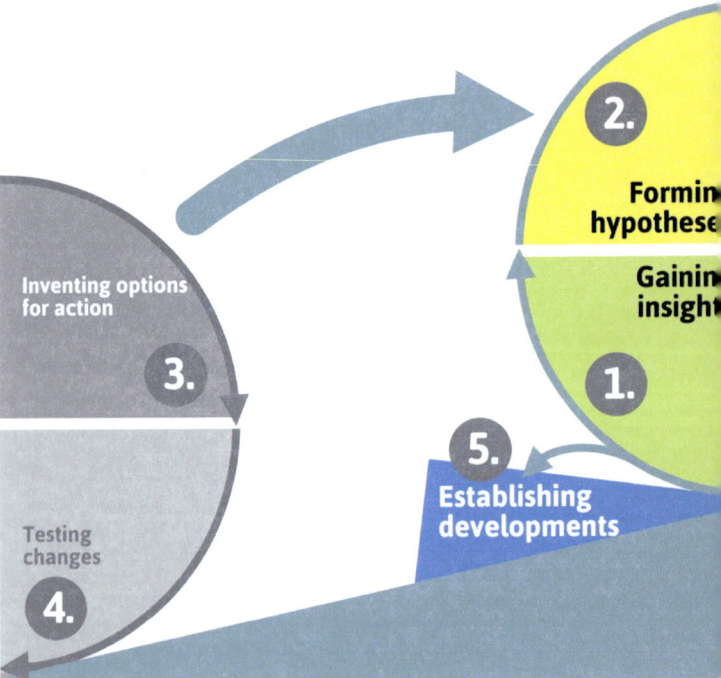

Fig. 1: Agile OE loop

3. INVENTING OPTIONS FOR ACTION

The selected hypotheses guide us to identify potential courses of action. What kind of changes do we want to test and in which experimental framework in order to develop the organisation in the way we envisage (increasing resources and system stability)? We do not assume causal results, but place

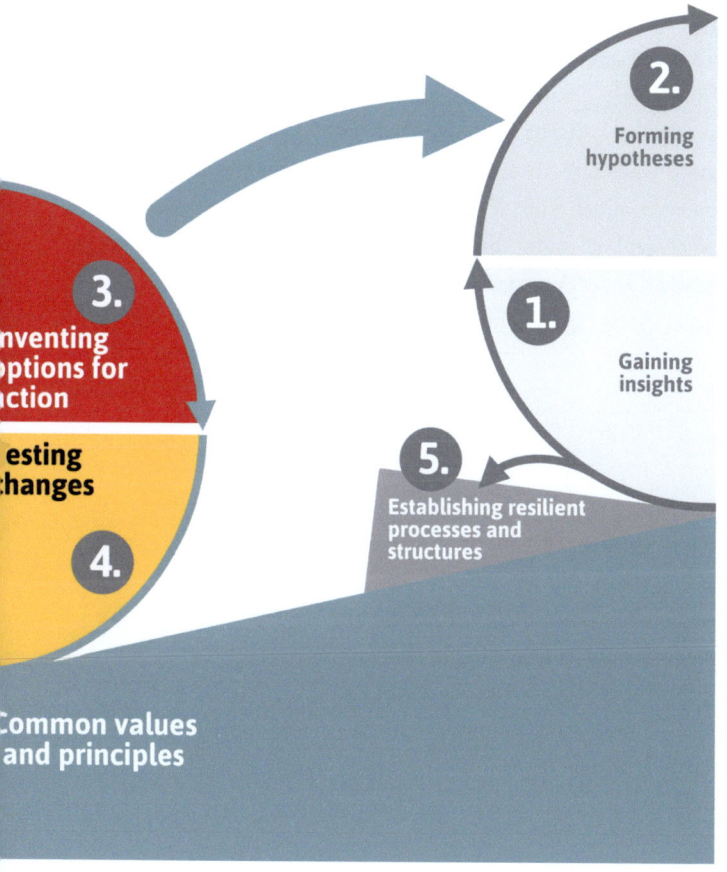

3.
nventing
ptions for
ction

esting
changes

4.

2.
Forming
hypotheses

1.
Gaining
insights

5.
Establishing resilient
processes and
structures

Common values
and principles

our ideas for change in the context of the hypotheses we have chosen. As far as possible, the changes are not irreversibly and extensively introduced, but limited in time and organisation, for example to certain products, processes, teams, locations, terms/shifts, etc.

4. TESTING CHANGES

The next step is try out and implement the change idea or ideas. The experimental framework also determines who initiates and takes responsibility for which changes and who is involved beyond that. The preparation of the experiments also includes considerations and, if necessary, concrete stipulations as to when and by whom the benefits of the experiment can be examined and assessed and when it is completed. With the evaluation of the experiment, the circle begins again to gain insights.

5. ESTABLISHING DEVELOPMENTS

An experiment is a special situation with selected framework conditions and participants in a protected and safe space. Being successful in this context is one thing; integrating and establishing the demonstrated and newly gained skills in the organisation in a sustainable way independently of the individual is another thing altogether.

To this end, these skills must be further anchored in the structures, processes and skills of the organisation. All participants must be able to reproduce the use cases reliably. And this is true not only for trivial cases, but for all the diversity and adversities of everyday work. It is about standardisation within the organisation.

This is the wedge jammed in visualised agile OE loop to prevent roll back: organisational development should not be a futile Sisyphean task.

COMMON VALUES AND PRINCIPLES

In all of this, especially in the formation of hypotheses and the invention of options for action, the participants are guided by their values and principles. Becoming aware of them, questioning them critically and reflecting on them, can promote the maturity of an organisation and its members.

EMPIRICAL AND OPEN-ENDED DEVELOPMENT

The agile OE cycle describes an iterative-empirical procedure. Accordingly, we do without long-term intervention architectures or project plans. Many organisational developments are understood as goal-oriented projects. The goals are usually set by a central client and linked to specific target criteria and values. Accordingly, the resulting changes can then be classified as right or wrong, quantified and become part of speculative investment calculations.

We contrast this with an open-ended approach. It is helpful to agree on desired results,

- as long as all stakeholders can wait in humility for the actual result,

- as long as everyone has the inner willingness to accept what is actually happening as reality and to learn from it.

- and as long as everyone is prepared to adapt and prepare for unexpected results.

The willingness to be open to results is an important addition to the principle of step-by-step development and merely an alternative way of looking at the principle of empirical development.

In doing so, we orientate ourselves towards the temporal possibilities of the organisation and its employees for leadership and organisational development work.

3

COLLEGIALLY DISTRIBUTED AND PULLING LEADERSHIP

Collegial leadership means that management work is performed dynamically and decentrally by many colleagues (according to the pull principle). This contrasts with centralised leadership by exclusive managers (according to the push principle).

In the context of collegial leadership, we do not understand leadership as an exclusive activity of executives, in which work and decisions are distributed by instruction or target agreement. Instead, we use the term leadership work to emphasize that leadership can be a natural and integral part of the work of any colleague.

Leadership is necessary, including hierarchical leadership. But who takes on what leadership work and when also depends on who is currently available, suitable and has sufficient knowledge, ability, trust and interest.

For predictable and regularly recurring leadership work and decisions, areas of responsibility are created in the form of roles or circles and their role holders are regularly redefined by colleagues.

Interested colleagues can be empowered by their colleagues on a case-by-case basis for spontaneously arising decision-making needs and concerns. If the culture of trust allows it or the situation requires it, colleagues may also empower themselves on the basis of shared values and principles. There are also simple principles which apply to (leadership) work that no one wants to do, but which is important. However, for reasons of space we will not go into detail of this here.

Attention is not only focused on decision-making and leadership needs, but also on tensions and issues of every kind for which responsibility has still not been assigned. A wait then follows to see who withdraws such issues or to see whether they are perhaps less important than originally thought.

ORGANISATIONAL DEVELOPMENT
AS META-MANAGEMENT IN PROGRESS

We therefore apply two different principles in parallel. What is predictable is distributed in advance and anchored in roles, structures and processes. The unpredictable is negotiated on a case-by-case basis with the help of fixed metaprocesses. Since we apply both principles to both operational content (work in the system) and to the organisational level (work on the system), organisational development simply becomes part of continuous meta-management. We do not have to separate these at all.

Hierarchical structures are needed to enable a large number of people to cooperate in the way they wish. The difference between collegial leadership and leadership with permanent managers in a line organisation is that the areas of responsibility can be further developed and renegotiated by the participants themselves.

THE PULL PRINCIPLE: ELICITING RESPONSIBILITY FROM A VACUUM

Many development processes are based on the pressure principle (push principle), in which the decision about what is to be done next is made by a different person or role than the one who has to implement it: the brain is at the top, the brawn at the bottom. Those who are given the task of implementing ideas regularly receive more work than the brain could handle on its own. Bottlenecks lead to overpressure.

Because this approach separates thinking and decision making from action and implementation, there is a systematic loss of responsibility. Those implementing decisions always feel responsible for their immediate results, but not for their significance in higher level contexts. And although managers are hierarchically responsible for their decisions, they regularly try to attribute their responsibility to the implementing persons.

Tasks can be distributed and assigned to others. Responsibility, in contrast, can only be taken. Anyone who tries to pass responsibility on to others nevertheless remains responsible until the recipient has decided to accept such responsibility. This is something that all managers know full well. Executives then complain that their employees do not assume any responsibility. These complaints and admonitions are nothing more than appeals. The transfer of responsibility is an agreement between people. It doesn't work if the recipient doesn't have the appropriate attitude or refuses to accept responsibility.

The pull principle, on the other hand, is based on the unity of thinking and acting or in other words of decisions and implementation. The implementing role-owner decides. He takes on new work as soon as he has the capacity to do so again. In turn, he makes the results of his work available for further processing in subsequent work steps. Kanban is a prime example of the pull principle. The workflow is considered here from beginning to end.

Suction is created by producing a vacuum. When this happens, responsibility is not distributed or pushed on to someone. Instead, opportunities for work and responsibility come to the attention of a person who can then decide to take them on. Work calls. The more it calls, the stronger the vacuum becomes and the more difficult it becomes for the people who perceive and feel this to avoid it.

This is why it is so important that, as far as possible, work is not assigned but is directly perceptible to the right people. A co-worker who receives a complaint directly from the customer can hardly withdraw from the issue and the pull it creates. An abstract announcement at the place of work about the current complaint rate does not generate a comparable physical reaction.

The pull principle is elementary, indispensable and irreplaceable for an agile organisation. Proactive self-organisation is only achievable if the pull principle can be implemented in appropriate structures and processes.

DIVERSE DEVELOPMENT

The principle of experimental development already promotes a certain diversity in developments. Instead of thinking, planning and calculating for a long period, an agile organisation tries out possibilities within a limited framework and only then decides what should be maintained or expanded. The decision-making threshold is lower because the consequences are initially more limited. An idea only needs to be good enough for it to be tried out. The ensuing investment and risks are acceptable.

In a complex environment in which it is impossible to determine with certainty, comprehensively or in good time which change is the right one, a greater diversity of experiments increases the likelihood of finding significant developments. Focused communication between different organisational units about their respective experiences with different approaches and solutions is useful. For example, a circle or business unit may try a different way of selecting personnel or planning shifts than one or two others. At the end of the trial phase, each circle reflects and evaluates its experiences, presents them to the others and thus facilitates a more qualified decision, change or even convergence towards a common standard.

4

DIALOGICAL PROCESS DEVELOPMENT

Although we would like to clearly identify and make visible responsibilities and areas of responsibility, it is also important that the persons involved and affected have a trusting and resilient working relationship.

All organisational development measures have greater or lesser effects on the work of some, sometimes very many, colleagues. When responsibilities and processes change, some colleagues relinquish responsibilities or tasks and others take them on. Some colleagues are empowered or given special decision-making powers. We would like to understand these transfers and authorisations as a dialogical process which takes place in different and mostly moderated communication formats as shown, for example, in the illustrated context bridge.

Responsibility can be formally transferred and changed quickly; at the relationship level it usually requires mutual trust. If you take on responsibility again or try something new, it means that your colleagues or previous managers

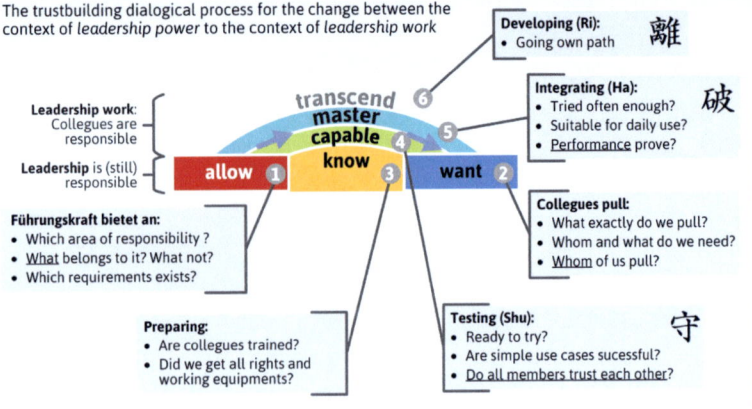

Context Bridge

The trustbuilding dialogical process for the change between the context of *leadership power* to the context of *leadership work*

Developing (Ri):
• Going own path　離

Integrating (Ha):
• Tried often enough?　破
• Suitable for daily use?
• Performance prove?

transcend ⑥
master
capable ④ ⑤
know ③　want ②

Leadership work: Colleagues are responsible
Leadership is (still) responsible

allow ①

Führungskraft bietet an:
• Which area of responsibility ?
• What belongs to it? What not?
• Which requirements exists?

Colleagues pull:
• What exactly do we pull?
• Whom and what do we need?
• Whom of us pull?

Preparing:
• Are collegues trained?
• Did we get all rights and working equipments?

Testing (Shu):
• Ready to try?　守
• Are simple use cases sucessful?
• Do all members trust each other?

Kommerzielle Nutzung bei Nennung des Rechteinhabers erlaubt: Bernd Oestereich, Claudia Schröder (https://kollegiale-fuehrung.de/)

Fig. 2: Context bridge for the change from leadership power to leadership work

have confidence in you. The person's new actions are observed by others and trustworthiness is verified and evaluated: Does the person do justice to the task? Does he/she do it well enough? How can we give him/her appropriate support?

The responsible person can also ask herself questions such as: What else do I need? How do the others rate my work? Am I satisfied myself?

The better contact there is between all the participants and the better they discuss such questions, clarify their expectations, provide case-related feedback and identify possible tensions, the easier and more quickly the change can succeed.

As we no longer see organisational development in terms of large projects, but as a constant flow of small elementary experiments, the expectations, attributions and responsibilities are less diffuse and can refer to individuals or at least to very few people.

EMPOWERING DEVELOPMENT

There are still many prejudices against self-organisation. It is said to lead to completely inefficient and exhaustingly endless discussions. Majority decisions have a reputation for producing mediocrity.

The principle is therefore not to make any content decisions in teams or groups, but instead to determine the person or persons who then decide on the content.

Self-empowerment is justifiable if self-empowered actions take place in small and manageable steps and the actions and results are systematically reflected upon in order to learn from them together. Self-empowerment begins with courage and trust in the other. The degree of trust given determines the extent of the self-empowered steps. The common learning process usually confirms the advance and thus systematically creates new trust.

The more certain participants are of their common values and principles, the more resilient and courageous self-empowerment will be.

The prerequisite for this is genuine personal responsibility. This means that people who act independently must also be able to feel the immediate consequences of their actions. For example, if someone hires a new colleague or buys a new machine, he should have to work with the new colleague himself or use the machine himself.

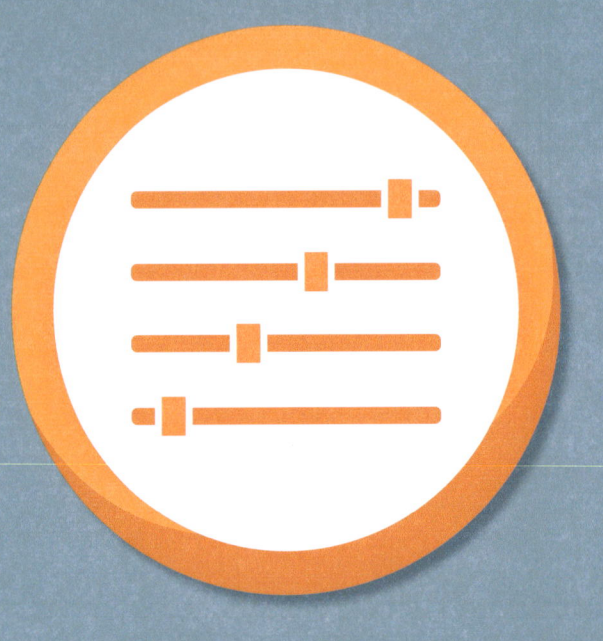

5

CLEAR FRAMEWORK CONDITIONS

As our approach is not based on replacing an existing management system with a new one, the coexistence and demarcation of different management systems is therefore relevant. We distinguish between:

- The existing own framework conditions: What is self-designable and what is given?

- Cooperative relationships with areas that are organised according to other leadership principles.

Each guide system is embedded or respectively has to be embedded in a defined frame. The topmost framework is defined by the partners (owners) and regulated in the articles of association of the company and the management contracts. For example, which transactions are subject to approval by the shareholders' meeting. This is mostly followed by a multi-level, hierarchical subdivision into areas of responsibility.

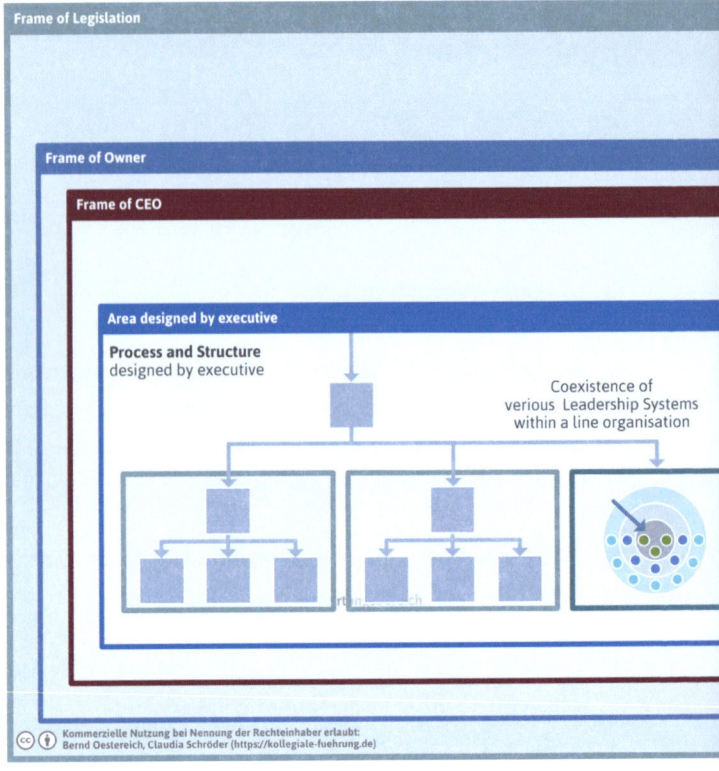

Fig. 3: Clear Framework conditions

For collegial leadership, we define the framework conditions in the form of a delegation matrix which describes which areas of responsibility and leadership aspects can be shaped by collegial leadership as well as whether and how far they have already been adapted by the collegial leadership.

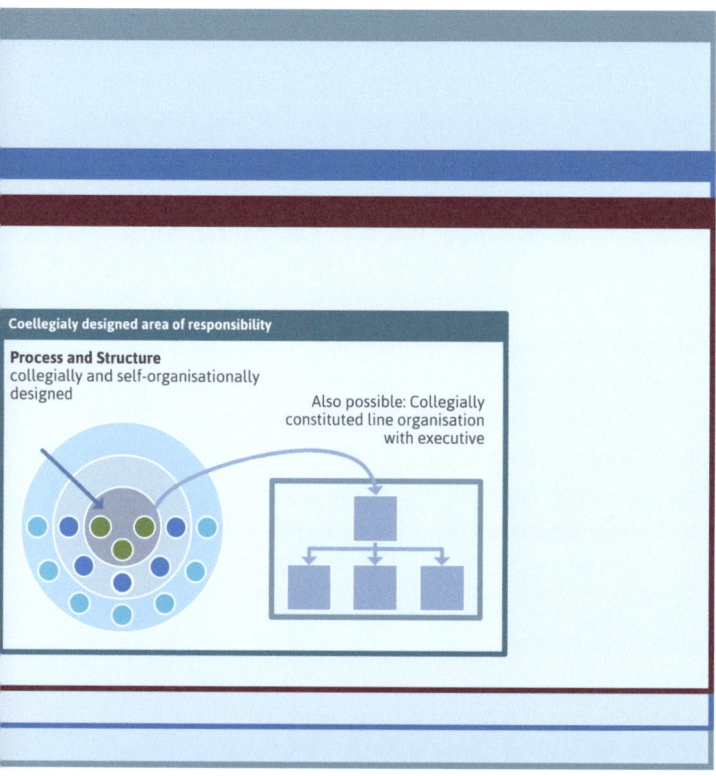

Coellegialy designed area of responsibility

Process and Structure
collegially and self-organisationally designed

Also possible: Collegially constituted line organisation with executive

In addition, each management area must be able to cooperate with areas which are organised according to different principles and patterns, such as line organisation, project organisation, etc. The best known example of how different management systems are linked is therefore the matrix organisation.

There is usually disciplinary leadership by superiors in a line organisation orthogonal (right-angled) to content leadership in a project organisation by project leaders or similar.

Communication takes place between areas that are managed and structured according to different patterns. This is not usually a problem if the areas of responsibility are reasonably clear and well known and provided that they do not act contradictorily (which is unfortunately structurally provoked in many matrix organisations) and contact persons, i.e. explicit interface managers, who are named. In this respect, cooperation between members of a collegially managed division and members of a line organisation also takes place in a familiar manner.

CONTEXTUAL MARKING

The coexistence of different management and organisational systems works all the better, the easier it is for all participants to know the context in which they find themselves and the issues with which they are currently concerned: Where do which rules and principles apply?

Just as the same people show different behaviours in different contexts (people behave quite differently in a football stadium, for example, than they do in a theatre) so also may quite different behaviours and cultures become apparent in an organization's different sub systems and contexts. People's behaviour depends more on their context than on their personality.

The change from a line organisation to a collegial organisation can take place slowly and gradually and thus result in the temporary or permanent coexistence of the two systems. In this case, it is very important that colleagues are able to distinguish the valid context.

6

CLEAR INTERNAL STRUCTURE
AND PROCESS SPECIFICATIONS AT THE START

START OF META PROCESSES

No matter what stage of development an organisation is at the moving forward and explorative step-by-step model enables it to develop further systematically, learn and improve itself. But how does an organisation actually manage to put this model into operation and start applying it?

We solve this chicken and egg problem by proposing concrete starting practices as consultants or initiators. A common suggestion at the beginning is the leadership monitor, as described in more detail in our book. In addition, there are numerous other possible starting practices. Much more important than the question of how good the initial proposal is, however, is the fact that a concrete proposal exists at all. Otherwise, the organisation would fall into a vacuum. Self-organisation would lead to people being left on their own. Colleagues would be completely overwhelmed as they would not know what they should do to organise themselves. Self-organisation should begin with organisation before the self dominates.

In order to avoid unnecessary group-dynamic processes, self-organisation begins with an act of external organisation. This may at first sound paradoxical. But what is decisive is, that practices proposed from outside include a learning loop so that the adaptation also includes the initially proposed practices.

PRE-TRAINING?

An alternative could be to train the relevant colleagues and enable them to develop their own competent proposals first. However, this is a much more expensive approach which costs more time, money and nerves, and may nevertheless not produce comparable results.

We therefore consider it more advisable to have continuous learning guidance to help the colleagues involved develop basic communicative skills.

CLEAR STARTING SITUATIONS EVEN ON A SMALL SCALE

Just as we strive for a high level of process and structural security when introducing agile organisational and leadership principles, we also try this on a small scale, for example when new circles or roles are constituted. Each circle needs a name, a purpose, a clear list of members (membership), a minimum number of roles for self-organisation and a minimum number of work meetings or processes to ensure the basic working capacity of the circle.

MORE ABOUT THE AUTHORS

As entrepreneurs, Claudia Schröder and Bernd Oestereich are pioneers for agile methods and collegially managed organisations. After having gained experience in their own companies they have been able to inspire many other entrepreneurs with their knowledge. Beneath that they qualify external organisational companions and in-house coaches for collegial organisations.

Their book, «Das kollegial geführte Unternehmen - Ideen und Praktiken für die agile Organisation von morgen», published in 2016, is a bestseller reference book and standard work on the subject also as their second book, «Agile Organisationsentwicklung – Handbuch zum Aufbau anpassungsfähiger Organisatonen», published in November 2019.

Additional download material you will find here:
https://kollegiale-fuehrung.de/

IMPRINT

©Claudia Schröder, 2020
Production and Publisher, BoD – Books on Demand, Norderstedt, Germany
ISBN 978-3-7519-6697-9

Layout: Claas Möller, www.claasbooks.de
Illustrations: Melina Pink, www.melina.pink
Sketchnote: Heike Heeg, www.c-hochdrei.de
Graphics: Bernd Oestereich and Claudia Schröder

Bibliographical Information of the German National Library (»Deutsche Nationalbibliothek«):
The German National Library records this publicaton in the German National Library (»Deutsche Nationalbibliografie«).

Detailed bibliographical data can be found under http://dnb.dnb.de